# MAYER SMITH

# Heartbound by the Moon's Curse

*First edition*

This book was professionally typeset on Reedsy.
Find out more at reedsy.com

# Contents

# One

# Binding

The night smelled of blood and fire.

Cassian tightened his grip on the hilt of his sword, the steel slick with the sweat of his palm. The battlefield was silent now, the echoes of steel on steel replaced by the eerie hush of the dead. Smoke curled from smoldering ruins, twisting into the night air like spectral fingers, and above it all—hanging unnaturally large in the sky—was the moon.

Red. Swollen. Watching.

His breath came shallow as he turned, scanning the bodies strewn across the temple ruins. He hadn't wanted this fight, hadn't sought this war, yet fate had dragged him into it, chaining him to a prophecy he didn't understand. The order had been clear—drive out the remaining cultists who had sought refuge in the temple of the fallen goddess, wipe away any lingering trace of the celestial heresy.

He had expected zealots. He had expected bloodshed.

He had not expected her.

At the center of the ruins, where the moonlight pooled like spilled wine, a woman lay crumpled on the broken stone altar. Her dark hair spread around her in tangled waves, her arms slack at her sides as if she had been cast from the heavens themselves.

Cassian's pulse pounded as he took a step closer.

She was unlike any woman he had ever seen. Skin as pale as moonlight, lips stained a bruised red. A golden sigil shimmered across her collarbone, shifting like liquid under the moon's glow. Chains—celestial, not mortal—bound her wrists to the ruined altar, inscribed with prayers long forbidden by the gods.

He knew, without needing to be told, who she was.

Selene. The exiled goddess of the moon.

His heart should have filled with dread, but instead, there was something else—a pull, deep and visceral, as though an unseen thread had knotted itself around his soul.

Her eyes fluttered open.

Cassian stepped back. A mistake.

The moment his foot scraped against the stone, her gaze snapped to him—ancient, storm-laden, filled with a knowledge that did not belong in this mortal world.

"You…" Her voice was a breath, a whisper lost in the wind, yet it struck him like a blade.

Cassian hesitated. Every instinct screamed at him to leave, to turn back before the weight of something far greater than himself crashed down upon him. But he could not move.

The moon pulsed above them.

Selene inhaled sharply, and the air seemed to shudder around her. Then, the chains binding her wrists cracked, a sound like thunder splitting the sky.

A great force slammed into Cassian's chest. He staggered, gasping, his vision going white-hot as something unseen wrapped around him, burning through his skin, through his bones.

A curse.

His knees hit the ground, his breath strangled in his throat as the invisible force wove itself into his body, binding him to something vast and incomprehensible. His pulse stuttered, his veins turning ice-cold, then molten hot, as the power settled deep inside him like a second heart.

Then, silence.

Cassian panted, his hands braced against the cold stone. His vision swam, but through the haze, he saw Selene standing now, rubbing her wrists where the chains had been. Her eyes locked onto his—no longer just storm-filled, but something more.

Knowing.

He swallowed hard. "What... have you done?"

Selene lifted her chin, her expression unreadable.

"I have done nothing," she murmured. "The gods have bound us."

Cassian's stomach twisted. He could feel it—the invisible tether between them, the way her presence now brushed against his soul like the pull of the tide. He tried to move, to stand on unsteady feet, but the moment he did, pain flared in his chest like a thousand burning needles.

He froze. It wasn't his pain. It was hers.

His gaze snapped to her. She watched him, her expression strangely calm despite the storm raging in her eyes.

"We are cursed now, you and I," she said softly. "Where you go, I will go. Where I suffer, you will suffer."

Cassian clenched his fists, his pulse hammering in his ears.

"No," he bit out. "This isn't possible."

Selene let out a breath that might have been a laugh, except there was no humor in it.

"You think I wished for this?" she whispered. "You think I wanted to be bound to a mortal?"

He flinched at the venom in her words. He should have been furious, should have been reaching for his sword, for an answer, for anything but the weight of her presence inside his soul.

But beneath her anger, he saw something else.

Fear.

His mind reeled. The gods had done this? Why? What purpose could they have in chaining a celestial to a mortal knight?

And what would it mean for them both?

The moon above them pulsed again, and a whisper—low and cruel—brushed against the edges of his mind.

It has begun.

A shiver rolled down his spine. He did not know who had spoken.

But he knew, without a doubt, that they were no longer alone.

Selene turned sharply, her gaze darting beyond the ruins, toward the forest beyond. Cassian followed her stare. At first, there was nothing—only the wind whispering through the scorched trees.

Then, the shadows moved.

Cassian's hand went to his sword, even as a cold dread settled in his gut.

The gods had bound them.

And now, something had come to collect.

# Two

# Knight's Oath

T he pain came first.

Cassian barely had time to register the icy grip twisting through his chest before he staggered, his knees buckling against the cold stone floor. His sword slipped from his grasp, clattering against the ruins with a sharp, metallic ring. His body seized as if something unseen had wrapped its fingers around his ribs and squeezed.

He gasped.

Selene sucked in a breath at the same time.

The goddess stood rigid a few paces away, clutching her stomach as if she had been struck. Moonlight carved sharp lines against her pale skin, highlighting the tension in her face.

Her lips parted in a silent gasp, her fingers trembling.

Cassian clenched his jaw. Not just his pain. Hers.

His pulse thundered in his ears. The invisible thread that had woven itself between them was real—tangible in the way his agony was now hers, in the way her presence coiled inside his soul like a brand seared into flesh.

Selene exhaled shakily. "Damn them," she whispered. "Damn the gods to their own void."

Cassian forced himself to his feet, breathing through the residual ache. His body felt… altered. Not weaker, but different. Like something deep within him had been reshaped in ways he could not yet name.

"You knew this could happen," he accused, voice rough.

Selene shot him a glare, her silver eyes flashing with something dark. "I knew nothing. I am no more their puppet than you are."

Cassian's lips curled in frustration. "Then why have they bound us?"

Selene's silence stretched between them, heavy as the cursed moon above.

Cassian stepped forward, closing the space between them. He could hear her shallow breaths, could see the tension lingering in the curve of her shoulders. Up close, she was more striking than she had any right to be—her beauty otherworldly, but edged with sorrow, with fury, with something unbreakable.

And yet, despite her defiance, something fragile flickered in her expression.

A woman cast from the heavens. A goddess shackled in mortal chains.

Cassian exhaled sharply, stepping back. Don't be a fool. She is not yours to pity.

The ruins around them had fallen eerily silent. The wind had stilled. Even the night creatures that had sung their distant songs were absent now, as if the world itself had recoiled from what had happened here.

Selene's fingers ghosted over her wrist, where the celestial chains had bound her just moments ago. "The gods do not act without reason," she murmured, more to herself than to him. "This binding is no accident."

Cassian flexed his fingers, ignoring the lingering throb in his chest. "Then how do we break it?"

Selene's expression twisted with something unreadable. "Breaking a celestial curse is no small feat. If there is a way, it will not come without cost."

Her words unsettled him, but before he could press further, a sound echoed through the ruins.

A slow, deliberate footstep.

Cassian's instincts flared. His hand was on his sword in an instant, even before his gaze flicked toward the shadows at the edge of the temple ruins. We are not alone.

Selene's spine straightened. She heard it too.

Another step. Then another.

A figure emerged from the darkness. Cloaked, hooded, moving with an eerie, inhuman grace. Though its face was obscured, Cassian could feel its gaze—cold and knowing, pressing against his skin like a blade.

Selene stiffened beside him. "A celestial emissary," she murmured.

Cassian's grip on his sword tightened. One of the gods' messengers. He had heard the tales—whispers of their presence at moments of divine reckoning, of their cold, impartial judgment. They did not intervene unless the gods willed it.

Which meant this was no coincidence.

The figure stopped a few feet away, its cloak stirring despite the windless night. When it spoke, its voice was hollow, like something speaking through a thousand echoes.

"Bound."

Cassian braced himself, his pulse pounding against his ribs. "Who are you?"

The emissary tilted its head slightly, as if examining them both. "A servant of the divine. I have come to bear witness."

Selene's voice was sharp. "Bear witness to what?"

A pause. Then—

"To the first step of your undoing."

The air turned thick. Suffocating.

Cassian shifted closer to Selene, though he did not know why. Perhaps it was instinct, the unconscious need to shield something fragile from an unseen predator. Or perhaps it was the binding, the unnatural thread that now tethered them, making him feel her unease as though it were his own.

The emissary continued, its voice dripping with something too calm to be comforting. "The gods have set this path before you. Your binding is fate. To resist it is to resist the will of the divine."

Selene's jaw clenched. "Then why send you? What do they fear?"

The emissary did not answer. Instead, it lifted a hand from the folds of its cloak, revealing a shimmering piece of parchment.

A decree.

Cassian recognized the celestial script, though he could not read its meaning. But the moment his eyes landed on it, something deep within him understood.

Selene paled beside him.

"They demand we fulfill the binding," she whispered.

Cassian's fingers tightened around his sword. "What does that mean?"

Selene tore her gaze from the decree and met his eyes. There was something there he didn't like. Something like resignation.

"It means we are no longer our own," she said softly. "The gods have marked us as theirs."

Cassian's blood ran cold.

He had spent his life fighting for his kingdom, believing that his choices were his own. And yet here, now, the truth pressed against his ribs like an iron brand.

He was no longer just a knight. She was no longer just a fallen goddess.

They were something else.

Something cursed.

The emissary's voice cut through the silence once more.

"The binding will demand sacrifice."

A gust of wind swept through the ruins, scattering the ash and embers across the temple stones. When Cassian blinked, the emissary was gone.

But the decree remained, floating gently to the ground between them, glowing faintly under the cursed moon.

Cassian swallowed hard. "I don't like this."

Selene let out a breath that sounded too much like a sigh of defeat. "Nor do I."

For the first time, she looked at him—not as a goddess, not as a burden, but as something closer to an equal. Someone shackled to the same fate, whether they willed it or not.

Cassian's throat tightened.

The gods had bound them.

And now, they would demand their due.

# Three

# Knight's Oath

The night was not silent.

The wind curled through the ruins, carrying the echoes of something unseen—whispers just beyond Cassian's reach. They wove through the scorched temple stones, slithering like smoke, hollow and thin, like voices speaking from another realm.

Cassian tightened his grip on his sword. He was no stranger to battle, to the presence of an unseen enemy lurking just out of reach. And yet, this was different.

This was something he could not fight.

The celestial decree still lay between them, glowing with a faint, unholy shimmer. The words were written in a language Cassian could not read, yet the moment he set eyes upon them, a cold truth pressed against his mind: The gods had claimed them. There would be no escape.

Selene hadn't moved since the emissary disappeared.

She stood motionless, her eyes locked onto the decree, her expression unreadable. But beneath the impassive mask, Cassian could sense something unraveling within her.

Panic.

Anger.

And something far worse—fear.

Cassian exhaled through his nose, forcing his own unease into the pit of his stomach. "Tell me you have a way out of this."

Selene didn't look at him. "If I did, I would have taken it already."

His patience thinned. "Then what does it mean? This decree—this 'binding'? The emissary said we had to fulfill it. What does that mean for us?"

At last, she turned to him.

The moonlight caught the silver in her eyes, making them almost glow. Her expression was calm, too calm. But he wasn't fooled—he had seen warriors wear the same look before a battle they knew they wouldn't win.

She took a slow step toward him, her fingers brushing the edges of the parchment. "The gods are playing a game. We are pieces on their board, and this decree is their move."

Cassian frowned. "You're speaking in riddles."

She let out a quiet, humorless laugh. "Because the truth is a riddle, knight." Her fingers traced over the glowing script, her brows knitting together in thought. "A celestial binding is an ancient magic, meant to chain one soul to another. It is not given lightly. It is not done without purpose."

Cassian swallowed, a pit forming in his gut. "Why us?"

Selene lifted her gaze to his. "Because they need us to fulfill something that only we can."

He scoffed. "That doesn't answer anything."

Selene's fingers curled into a fist, frustration flashing in her expression. "It means, Cassian, that the gods want something neither of us would willingly give."

Cassian studied her, watching the way her shoulders tensed, the way she averted her gaze ever so slightly. She knows more than she's saying.

He took a step closer. "What aren't you telling me?"

Silence stretched between them.

For a moment, he thought she wouldn't answer. Then—

"The last time a celestial binding was performed," she said slowly, "it was to forge a weapon."

A chill slithered down Cassian's spine. "A weapon?"

Selene nodded once, the moonlight catching the edges of her sharp features. "Two souls, bound by divine law, forced into servitude. Their fates entwined, their pain shared, their wills no longer their own." Her voice was bitter, edged with something close to hatred. "The gods do not forge bindings to be kind. They do it to control."

Cassian felt the weight of her words settle over him. A shackle he had not seen before.

"So we're slaves," he said flatly.

Selene's expression darkened. "No," she whispered. "We are something worse."

The wind howled through the temple ruins, and the whispers rose again, curling around them like unseen fingers. Cassian tensed, instinctively stepping closer to Selene, his body reacting before his mind had even registered it.

And then—

A new presence stirred.

Not an emissary.

Not a god.

Something in between.

Cassian turned sharply, his sword already half-drawn, but Selene's hand shot out, gripping his wrist before he could unsheath it fully.

"Wait."

He glanced at her, his pulse hammering, but she wasn't looking at him.

Her gaze was fixed on the temple's shattered archway, where a figure now stood.

Tall. Cloaked in shadow. Its face obscured beneath the hood of its robe, the fabric shifting like living smoke. The presence that rolled off of it was suffocating—not quite mortal, not quite divine.

Cassian had spent his life fighting enemies of flesh and blood. But this? This was something else.

Selene's grip on his wrist tightened.

The figure took a step forward. The ground beneath it seemed to shudder in response.

"I bring an offer," it said, its voice like rusted metal scraping against stone. "One that will save you from your suffering."

Cassian's pulse slammed against his ribs.

An offer.

From the gods? Or something worse?

Selene's breath was steady, but her hand on his wrist trembled ever so slightly.

"Speak," she commanded.

The figure's hood shifted slightly, though no face could be seen beneath it. "The binding cannot be undone."

Cassian's stomach dropped. He had expected the answer, but hearing it aloud made it feel more like a cage snapping shut.

"There is no breaking what the gods have forged," the figure continued. "But there is a way to ease the burden."

Cassian narrowed his eyes. "How?"

The figure did not move. "One of you must submit."

Silence.

Cassian glanced at Selene, but she was already staring at the figure with icy detachment. "Submit?" she echoed.

"The gods do not wish to control two unwilling vessels," the figure said. "One must surrender their will. One must bow, so the other may lead."

Cassian stiffened. "You mean one of us must become the other's servant."

The figure inclined its head. "Yes."

His stomach twisted.

Selene was unreadable beside him, but he could feel the tension radiating from her. The weight of the choice pressing against them both.

The gods had left them no freedom. But now, they wanted them to choose who would wear the chains.

Cassian's hands curled into fists.

He would never bow.

And yet…

He glanced at Selene, at the way her silver eyes burned with defiance. The way her jaw had tightened, the way she refused to look at him.

She would never bow either.

The gods had set the game.

Now, they had to play.

Four

# The Hidden City

⚬⚬⚬

The night felt as though it were holding its breath.

Cassian could feel the weight of it pressing down on him, a suffocating quiet that clung to his skin like the dust of the ruins they had left behind. The path before them was dark, winding through a dense forest that seemed to stretch endlessly. Not a sound came from the trees, no rustling of leaves, no calls of nocturnal creatures. Just the soft crackle of their footsteps on the ground, and the occasional low murmur of Selene's breath beside him.

He kept his eyes forward, but his thoughts swirled in chaos. The figure in the temple had made its offer, its promise of salvation—or surrender. One must submit.

And the choice had been left to them.

Cassian clenched his jaw, his hand unconsciously resting near the hilt of his sword. He didn't trust the gods. And he didn't trust the figure, or the veiled words it had spoken. They wanted one of them to bow, to surrender to the binding—but which of them would choose?

He glanced sideways at Selene.

She was walking ahead of him, her back straight, her posture regal despite the evident weariness in her movements. Even now, despite everything, she looked like someone who belonged to the stars, someone who belonged beyond this world. Her dark hair fell around her like a curtain of night, and the moonlight made her skin glow faintly, as if it were not flesh but light itself.

Cassian's heart stuttered, but he forced the thought aside. Focus.

The path led them through the forest, and every step felt like an eternity. After the encounter with the emissary, Selene had not said a word, and Cassian hadn't pushed her. He knew she was struggling with something deeper than the curse. There was something more to this binding, something that she wasn't revealing, and he couldn't help but feel that the choice the figure had given them was far more than it seemed.

They had to reach the city of Ebonreach. There, they would find answers.

Or, so Selene had said.

Ebonreach was a place of legend, a city hidden beneath the roots of the earth, where ancient knowledge was kept from the prying eyes of mortals. The stories told of a forgotten race, of gods and mortals who once walked side by side, before the heavens fell silent and the world grew too small for what it had once been.

Cassian couldn't shake the feeling that they weren't just looking for answers. They were running from something—or perhaps being drawn into something far darker than they could ever imagine.

His mind turned to the gods. What did they want from him? From Selene?

He glanced over at her again, and this time she met his gaze. There was something in the look she gave him—something that held both warning and appeal, a silent invitation that made his pulse quicken.

She didn't speak, but there was a shift in the air around them. The tension between them had grown since the moment they had been bound by the curse, and Cassian wasn't sure if it was the gods or something else that made it unbearable. The air felt thicker when they were near each other, as if it couldn't contain the pull between them, like two magnetic forces tugging at each other.

"What happens when we get to Ebonreach?" he asked, his voice low.

Selene didn't answer immediately. Her gaze flicked ahead, scanning the path with quiet alertness. "We'll find the truth," she said finally, her voice tight. "The truth about the binding."

Cassian didn't ask her to elaborate. He could sense that there was more she wasn't saying, but it was not the time for questions. His instincts told him that. There was something more pressing in the air. A shift in the wind that hinted at danger.

Suddenly, Selene halted, causing Cassian to stop in his tracks behind her.

She had felt it too.

They stood in silence, surrounded by the dense, darkened trees. The moon above them hung heavy, casting long, sharp shadows across the path. The woods had grown unnervingly still, the quiet almost suffocating. Even the wind had stopped.

Cassian's grip on his sword tightened. "What is it?"

Selene's voice was barely a whisper. "We are being watched."

His heart skipped a beat. He knew it. He could feel it, too—the presence in the air, the oppressive weight of something lurking in the shadows. It was more than just the gods, more than just the curse. It was something deeper, older, a force beyond comprehension.

Before he could respond, the air crackled—like static, sharp and sudden—and then, as if the forest itself had turned against them, something moved.

A shadow darted across their path. Faster than any human, it blurred the edges of reality itself, its form too indistinct to discern. Cassian drew his sword in one smooth motion, his body already in battle stance, his senses on high alert.

Selene's eyes narrowed. She stepped forward, her hand raised to halt him. "Wait."

Cassian's instincts screamed at him to strike first, but he stayed his hand, though every muscle in his body screamed for action. His gaze flicked toward her, confusion in his eyes.

Selene's expression was unreadable, her silver eyes glowing faintly. "It's not a threat," she murmured.

Before he could respond, the shadow reappeared, slipping between the trees like a wisp of smoke. It was gone again almost before he could fully track its movement.

"What the hell was that?" Cassian breathed, unable to keep the edge of fear from his voice.

Selene's gaze never left the trees. "A watcher," she said. "An agent of the gods."

Cassian frowned. "An agent?"

"Yes," she replied, her voice heavy with something like regret. "The gods do not let their puppets wander far without their eyes upon them."

A chill ran down Cassian's spine. He had heard the rumors—of divine agents, creatures bound to the will of the gods, beings neither entirely mortal nor divine. The fact that they were already under watch only made the weight of their journey feel heavier.

The moment passed as quickly as it had come. The watcher, or whatever it was, was gone, leaving only the silence of the forest behind.

Selene exhaled slowly. "We must move quickly. Ebonreach is close, but the gods will not let us reach it easily."

Cassian didn't need her to explain. The weight of their path was already clear.

They continued down the narrow path, though the tension between them had shifted, thickened. The presence of the watcher lingered like a dark stain on their minds. Every step they took felt like an offering to the gods, as though they were walking toward something far more dangerous than they realized.

But there was something else that gnawed at Cassian—something deeper than the fear of the gods, the curse, or even the watcher.

It was the way Selene's presence wrapped itself around him like an unseen thread, drawing him closer, even as the bond between them stretched and strained, pulling them into a future neither of them could escape.

And no matter how he tried to suppress it, the feeling was there, a gnawing certainty that he couldn't shake.

She would be the death of him.

# the Betrayer

The path ahead was choked with fog.

Cassian stood at the edge of the forest clearing, his eyes scanning the shadowed landscape, his body tense, as if expecting an attack at any moment. The fog clung to the ground in thick, twisting tendrils, curling around the stone ruins and ancient trees like the fingers of some forgotten god. The moon overhead was half-obscured by dark clouds, its light flickering like a dying flame.

Beside him, Selene's presence was a constant pull at his senses, her near silence somehow louder than the howling wind that swept through the trees. She had not spoken since they left the woods behind, and her distance was palpable—like an invisible wall between them, one built not by her, but by something darker.

Something neither of them could control.

They had been traveling for days now, moving deeper into a land few mortals dared tread. The roads they walked were ancient, forgotten paths that led to the city of Ebonreach, the hidden sanctuary where Selene believed they would find answers—answers that might finally break the curse that bound them together. But with each step, something grew heavier in the air. The oppressive silence, the subtle weight that pressed against Cassian's chest, was more than just the threat of divine retribution. It was something else, something he couldn't place.

The forest had grown quiet again, as if even nature itself had paused to listen.

Cassian stole a glance at Selene. She was staring ahead, her gaze fixed, unblinking, as if she could see something that wasn't there. Her lips were pressed into a thin line, and though she held herself with the poise of a goddess, there was something fractured in the stillness of her expression.

For a moment, Cassian felt a flicker of sympathy for her—the same sympathy he had tried to bury since the day they were cursed together. But the feeling quickly dissolved, replaced by something far more dangerous. Trust.

He didn't trust her.

At least, he didn't trust the part of her that was bound to the gods.

"Selene," he said, his voice rough, breaking the silence. "You said Ebonreach would give us answers, but I'm starting to wonder if we're walking into something we can't escape."

She didn't respond immediately. Her fingers tightened around the hilt of her sword, her knuckles white against the dark leather.

"We are bound to something greater than ourselves," she finally said, her voice low, distant. "We always have been."

Cassian's stomach twisted. "That doesn't answer my question."

She met his gaze then, her eyes sharp, though there was something haunting in their depths. "It's not just the gods that control us, Cassian. There is something older, something beyond them. And it is coming for us."

His pulse quickened. "What are you talking about?"

Selene's jaw tightened, and for a moment, Cassian could have sworn he saw a flicker of fear in her eyes. But it was gone too quickly to be sure.

The moment stretched between them, thick with unspoken words. Cassian took a step closer, unable to help himself. He was drawn to her, despite the walls she had built between them. The curse, the gods, the lies—they all swirled together in his mind, and with every passing moment, the bond between them seemed to grow stronger, more suffocating.

"You're hiding something," he muttered.

"I'm not hiding anything." Her voice was almost a hiss, her eyes narrowing as she turned away from him, her attention focused on the fog ahead. "You wouldn't understand. None of this is meant for mortals."

A flash of anger surged in him, and before he could stop it, he grabbed her arm, spinning her to face him. "I don't care about the gods or their schemes, Selene. I care about the truth."

For a heartbeat, they stood there, chest to chest, her breath coming quick and sharp, his own pulse racing. The fog curled around them like an unseen force, thickening the air between them. Cassian could feel the pull of her presence, the weight of her gaze as it softened, just slightly. For a fleeting moment, there was no divine curse, no celestial plan—only two people, bound by something more than fate, something human.

But the moment shattered when the sound of footsteps broke the silence.

Heavy. Measured.

Cassian spun around, his hand instinctively going for his sword, but Selene stopped him with a single touch on his arm.

"Wait," she whispered. "It's not what you think."

Cassian's instincts were screaming at him. There was something wrong, something off about the way the fog was swirling, the way the shadows shifted at the edge of the clearing. He could feel the presence now—something unnatural, something dangerous.

A figure emerged from the mist.

It was cloaked in black, its features hidden beneath the shadow of its hood. But even from a distance, Cassian could feel the malice in the air, the coldness that seeped into his bones like ice. He instinctively stepped closer to Selene, his hand still on his sword, ready for whatever came next.

"Selene," the figure said, its voice smooth, like honey laced with venom. "It's been a long time."

Cassian froze. The voice... It wasn't just the malice that unsettled him—it was the recognition. The familiarity in the tone. He had heard it before, long ago, in the darkened halls of his childhood home.

The figure lowered its hood, revealing a face that sent a cold shiver through Cassian's spine.

It was a woman.

Her features were sharp, almost inhuman, with pale skin that seemed to shimmer in the fog. Her eyes were silver, like molten metal, glowing faintly in the dim light. But it wasn't her appearance that made Cassian's heart race—it was the recognition that churned in his chest, like a poison.

Nyx.

The Betrayer.

She was a name spoken in hushed tones, a legend among the celestial. Once a goddess, she had fallen from grace, her loyalty to the gods shattered when she defied them. But her betrayal had come at a great cost, and she had been cast down, never to return.

Until now.

Selene's voice was calm, but there was a dangerous edge to it. "What do you want, Nyx?"

The Betrayer smiled, and it was a smile that made Cassian's blood run cold. "What I want, Selene, is simple. You've made your choice, haven't you?"

Cassian's grip tightened on his sword. "You were one of them." His voice was low, the words like gravel in his throat. "You betrayed the gods. What do you want with us?"

Nyx's smile deepened, and there was something almost tender in the way she looked at Selene. "I was never one of them, Cassian. Not in the way you think." Her eyes flicked to him, and the expression on her face made his stomach turn. "You see, I was always meant to be something more."

Selene's shoulders stiffened, and Cassian could feel the tension radiating from her. There was history here, something that neither of them had revealed.

Nyx stepped closer, her voice dropping to a whisper. "The gods have always been afraid of what you two might become. And now… now they want to ensure you never find out."

Cassian's mind raced, his hand still resting on his sword. "What are you saying?"

Nyx's gaze flicked to him, and for a moment, there was something almost sad in her eyes. "You're not just pawns in their game, Cassian. You're something far worse. The gods know it. And they fear it."

Cassian's heart pounded. What had they become?

Nyx smiled again, her eyes glowing with an unholy light. "But I can help you. If you'll trust me."

Selene turned away, her voice low and steady. "You've already chosen your side, Nyx. And I've made mine."

For a moment, the forest was silent again, the fog swirling around them like a living thing. The betrayal that lingered between them was palpable, and Cassian could feel the weight of it settling on his chest.

But the choice, the choice they were all forced to make, hung in the air like a dark omen.

And neither of them could escape.

# Six

# The Mortal's Defiance

The silence that followed Nyx's departure felt unnatural. Cassian stood in the clearing, his breath shallow, his hand still wrapped around the hilt of his sword. Selene was beside him, her presence like a weight that pressed against his chest, though she didn't say a word. The fog still hung thick in the air, the moon casting a pale, sickly light over the scene as though it, too, was watching them with some malevolent interest.

Nyx had been a specter of the past, a shadow that had lingered just outside the realm of mortal knowledge. But now, her presence was a truth they couldn't ignore. The Betrayer. Cast out by the gods for defying them, and now, seemingly free— offering help that felt more like a threat than salvation.

Cassian's hand tightened on his sword, but he didn't draw it. He didn't need to. He could feel it—the danger that lingered in the air. The way the forest seemed to hold its breath, waiting.

"What did she mean?" Cassian finally asked, his voice low, as though speaking too loudly would make the silence shatter.

Selene didn't look at him. Her eyes were fixed on the ground in front of her, her expression unreadable. Her aura, usually so confident, was cracked now, jagged edges forming where calm once resided.

"I don't know," she said, her voice tight. "I've never trusted Nyx. Not fully."

Cassian narrowed his eyes. "She offered you something, didn't she? Help. To escape the gods. To break the curse."

Selene's jaw tightened, her fingers clenched at her sides. "I know what she offers. But it comes at a price. It always does."

The air around them thickened, heavy with unspoken truths. Cassian wanted to reach out to her, to shake the answers free, but something held him back. He couldn't put his finger on it—something about Selene's pain made his heart ache. She was too proud to show weakness, but he saw it now, beneath the layers of her defiance. He had seen enough in her eyes to know—she was hiding something.

But it was more than just her. It was them. The curse that bound them together. The gods. Nyx. The truth was slipping through his fingers like sand, and no matter how tightly he tried to grasp it, he couldn't make it hold.

"What if she's right?" he murmured, more to himself than to Selene. "What if we can't escape it? The curse… the gods… us?"

She glanced at him then, her silver eyes catching the flickering light of the moon.  There was something raw in her gaze—something that made him feel as if he were staring into the depths of an abyss.

"We can escape it," she said, her voice firm, though there was a tremor beneath the surface. "But we must do it on our terms. Not on hers. Not on the gods.'"

Her words settled in the air like the weight of a thousand storm clouds, thick with an intensity that made Cassian's chest ache. He didn't know what it was about her—her strength, her certainty, or the haunting sorrow beneath it all—but he felt himself drawn to her in a way that unsettled him.

"You're saying we defy the gods," he said softly, though it felt like an echo of something larger.

Her gaze softened, and for a moment, Cassian thought he saw something else there—trust. Not just the divine, twisted bond between them, but something real, something fleeting and fragile. It was there, and then it was gone, buried beneath the weight of their shared fate.

"We don't have a choice," she replied, her voice steady now. "The gods have made their move. We must make ours."

There was an edge to her words, as though she had already accepted the price they might have to pay. And that terrified him more than any of the gods could.

He was about to speak again when the sound of something cracking through the underbrush shattered the air.

Cassian's heart leapt in his chest. Instincts flared, his hand shooting to the hilt of his sword, but Selene was already moving—graceful, precise, her body a fluid blur of motion.

Something dark moved through the fog, shifting in and out of sight. A shadow. Unseen, but its presence was undeniable.

Cassian's pulse quickened. He wasn't sure whether it was the curse that made him feel the pull of danger so deeply, or if it was something else—something more primal, more raw. The way the air shifted, the way his body hummed with an unknown fear.

The figure stepped into view.

It was human, but it wasn't. Not entirely. The face was gaunt, the skin pale and stretched tight over the bones. The eyes—if they could be called eyes—were black as night, soulless and empty, as though the creature had never been alive to begin with.

It stepped forward, its movements jerky and disjointed. A doll, in the worst possible sense.

Cassian's grip tightened on his sword. "What in the gods' names—?"

The creature's head tilted to one side, its mouth opening wide, too wide. And then it spoke—its voice hollow, reverberating through the air like a sickened echo.

"You have been marked."

Cassian froze. The words weren't just spoken; they were felt—a deep, unshakable force that pressed against his chest, making his breath catch in his throat. He could feel it, that weight, that inevitable feeling of something creeping in, a flood of darkness closing in around him.

He stepped forward, ready to fight, but Selene's hand shot out to stop him.

"Don't," she warned, her voice cold, distant. "It's not alive. It's a shadow. A servant of the gods."

Cassian glanced at her, confusion flooding his chest. "Then what the hell is it doing here?"

Selene's gaze darkened. "Watching. Waiting. It knows our every move."

Cassian's stomach twisted. He didn't want to admit it, but he felt it too—that sense of being trapped. The gods were always one step ahead.

The shadow moved closer, and Cassian could feel its coldness seeping into his bones. The air around them seemed to drop a few degrees, the fog swirling more tightly, as if the entire world were holding its breath.

"The gods know we're close," Selene whispered. "They'll stop us at every turn. They'll make sure we can't reach Ebonreach. We cannot trust anything anymore."

The shadow spoke again, its voice like nails on glass. "The price must be paid."

Cassian clenched his fists. "What price?" he demanded, his voice rough with frustration.

But the shadow did not answer. Instead, it simply vanished, like a wisp of smoke slipping through the cracks of reality.

Silence descended once more, thick and suffocating.

Cassian stood there for a moment, staring into the empty space where the shadow had been. His heart raced, adrenaline still buzzing through his veins, and yet... there was something more—something heavier than fear.

It was anger.

He had been given no choice, no chance. The gods had woven their threads around him, and now, they expected him to be a puppet on their strings. And the worst part was—he was willing to fight.

But Selene, she seemed to have already resigned herself. She had already accepted the price they would pay.

Cassian's eyes flicked to her. She was staring ahead, her expression hard, her eyes cold. For a moment, he wondered if she, too, had already made her choice.

But as he stepped closer, there was something else in her gaze—a flicker of something he couldn't name. Fear. Fear not of the gods, but of what would come if they didn't fight back.

He reached out, his fingers brushing hers, and for a moment, the weight of their bond—of their shared curse—settled between them like an unspoken promise.

They had to fight.

And in that moment, Cassian realized—he would not let the gods win.

# Seven

# Dance of the Eclipse

The ballroom was alive with whispers.

Cassian stood at the edge of the great hall, his fingers tight around the crystal goblet in his hand. He hadn't wanted to come. He had no love for the fancy trappings of nobility, the glimmering dresses, the glittering masks, the hollow laughter of the privileged few who danced and reveled in the shadows of their gilded world.

But Selene had insisted.

"The city of Ebonreach hides more than just knowledge, Cassian," she had said, her voice soft yet commanding, the way only someone who had once been a goddess could speak. "The answers we seek are closer than you think. But we must blend in, must be seen."

She was right.  The ball was an opportunity, a masquerade where nobles from distant lands mingled with travelers and foreign dignitaries—an event that promised information about the binding that had cursed them. They had to be careful, and careful meant playing the game.

The room was a blur of color and movement, laughter cascading around them like a thousand droplets of rain. The masks that covered the faces of the attendees seemed to hide more than just their identities; they seemed to cloak their very souls, each one a barrier between the real world and the illusion of safety they had all created.

Cassian's eyes, however, were trained on one figure, one face that stood out in the crowd despite the secrecy of the evening. Selene.

She had disappeared into the crowd, her presence stilling the room like a gathering storm. She wore a gown of deep midnight blue, the fabric shimmering with every movement, and a mask that was both beautiful and haunting, the contours of her face hidden beneath silver filigree.  Her hair was loose, cascading like liquid night down her back. The way she moved—graceful, poised, as though every step were a dance of its own—captured everyone's attention.

But not his.

Cassian's eyes never left her, not even as the crowd shifted and swirled around him. His pulse quickened each time she glanced toward him, her silver eyes meeting his in fleeting, but potent, moments of shared understanding. They both knew why they were here, knew what was at stake.

But beneath it all, beneath the mission and the dangerous game they were playing, there was something else—a pull between them that neither of them had been able to resist.

Selene stepped gracefully into the center of the dance floor, and the music swelled, taking on a darker, more hypnotic rhythm. A prince from a far kingdom, his eyes hidden behind a gilded mask, stepped forward to ask her for a dance. The nobles watched, intrigued, as the two of them spun in perfect synchrony, their movements sharp, yet fluid, as if the world had bent to their will.

Cassian's grip on his goblet tightened. It wasn't just jealousy. He knew that. The thought of anyone else touching Selene— dancing with her like that—made his chest tighten in a way he couldn't explain.

But it was more than that.

As Selene moved in time with the prince, Cassian's heart raced for an entirely different reason. He couldn't quite place it— the feeling that something was wrong, that they were being watched. But this was not the first time tonight he had felt it. The shadows of the room seemed to press in on him, the air thick with unseen eyes, heavy with the weight of something sinister.

His gaze flicked around the room, searching for any sign of

movement, any hint of danger lurking in the corners. He had the unsettling sensation that the walls were closing in on him. The gods' influence was everywhere now, pulling at the edges of his mind, suffocating him with its quiet power. They were being watched, hunted like prey, and Cassian couldn't shake the feeling that the next step was already in motion.

A tap on his shoulder snapped him from his thoughts.

He turned sharply, instinctively ready to lash out, but stopped when his gaze landed on the figure before him.

Nyx.

She stood in front of him, her mask gleaming in the light, her expression as cold and calculating as always. Her presence in this place—the heart of the city, hidden away from the rest of the world—was both unnerving and expected.

"You are far from home, Cassian," she said, her voice dripping with mockery.

His hand curled into a fist at his side. "What do you want, Nyx?"

She smiled, but it was a smile that didn't reach her eyes. "Only to see how far you're willing to go to break free from your chains."

Cassian's heart skipped a beat. He could feel the weight of her words pressing against his chest, like something poisonous trying to make its way into his bloodstream.

"Don't," he muttered, his voice low. "I don't need your games."

"Oh, but you do," Nyx replied, her eyes flashing with something cold and ancient. "You don't even realize what you're up against, do you? You think the curse can be broken simply by your will. But there are forces in this world far older than the gods themselves." She leaned in closer, her lips brushing his ear as she whispered, "You're a fool to believe you have any control."

Cassian stiffened, his muscles tense, but before he could respond, the crowd shifted around him, and he saw something that froze his blood.

Selene.

But not the Selene he knew.

Her movements had slowed, her expression blank, as though a veil had descended over her face. She wasn't dancing anymore. The prince had stopped, his hand still on her waist, but it was the look in her eyes that made Cassian's stomach churn.

It wasn't the defiant, fire-laden gaze that she usually wore. It wasn't even the vulnerable look that sometimes flashed beneath her mask.

It was empty.

Her silver eyes were dull, staring at the prince as though he were the only person in the room, as though there was no one else—no one else—who mattered.

And then, just as suddenly, her gaze flicked to him.

Cassian's breath caught in his throat. There was something there, something distant, but it was enough to send a chill down his spine.

Something was wrong.

Without thinking, he shoved past Nyx, his heart pounding in his chest. He pushed his way through the dancers, through the revelry, and in that moment, the music seemed to fade, the laughter evaporating, leaving only the deafening sound of his pulse in his ears.

"Selene!"

Her eyes snapped back to him, the lifelessness fading as though she had snapped out of some trance.

She blinked once, twice, and then shook her head, as though trying to clear away the fog.

"What happened?" Cassian asked, his voice strained, his hand gripping her arm. "What did they do to you?"

Selene stared at him for a moment, as though she didn't quite recognize him. The fear in her eyes, the vulnerability—it wasn't her. It wasn't the woman he had been bound to, the woman who defied the gods at every turn.

"I—I don't know," she whispered, her voice shaky. "I just… I don't know."

Cassian's heart dropped. He wanted to ask more, to shake the answers from her, but the moment was broken by the sound of a laugh—a low, guttural chuckle that sent a ripple of unease through him.

Nyx.

She was standing in the corner of the room, watching them with that sick, satisfied smile.

"I warned you," she said, her voice low, taunting. "The gods are not so easily deceived."

Cassian's blood ran cold. He could feel the weight of her gaze on him, on Selene. She had done this. She had manipulated her, had forced her into that state—whatever it was. And the worst part?

Selene had almost—almost—fallen under its influence.

# Eight

# Chains of Fate

T he moon was full.

Cassian stood at the edge of the clearing, watching as the light bathed the forest in a cold, silvery glow. The trees stretched overhead like silent sentinels, their gnarled branches twisting against the sky. The air was thick, heavy with something he couldn't quite place—a pressure, as if the world itself were holding its breath.

Selene was beside him, her presence a quiet hum that seemed to vibrate in his chest. Her gaze was fixed on the horizon, her face unreadable beneath the dark mask she wore. She was beautiful—more than beautiful, something beyond the grasp of mere mortals—but it was the quiet sorrow in her eyes that unsettled him. The more he learned of her, the more he realized just how much she was hiding. How much they both were hiding.

It had been days since the masquerade, since Nyx had intervened in their lives again. The prince's strange influence on Selene, the trance she had nearly fallen into… it had left Cassian shaken, and yet, something deeper gnawed at him. He couldn't shake the feeling that they were drifting apart, despite the bond that bound them together.

The curse. The gods.

They were running out of time.

"I told you," Selene whispered, her voice low and distant, "I've never trusted Nyx. She has always had her own agenda. But she's not wrong about everything."

Cassian's gaze flicked to her. "What do you mean?"

She turned to face him then, her silver eyes catching the light of the moon, flashing with a quiet intensity. "There are forces beyond even the gods. The curse… it was never meant to be broken. It was meant to bind us. To use us."

Cassian's pulse quickened. "What do you mean? You said we could break it—"

"The curse was never meant for mortals like you and me to break," she said softly, her voice tight with a sorrow Cassian could almost taste. "We're just pawns in a game we don't understand, Cassian."

The weight of her words pressed down on him like a stone sinking into his chest.  His mind raced, but the truth—the terrible, suffocating truth—was already sinking in. The gods had created this curse to use them, to twist their fates into something neither of them could control.

"Then why are we still fighting?" he asked, his voice rough. "If it's all predetermined, if the gods are using us—why not just let it all go?"

She took a step forward, her presence pulling him closer like gravity.  Her fingers brushed against his, and for a fleeting moment, he felt the depth of her uncertainty. The bond between them was still raw, pulsing with energy, but it wasn't just the curse that kept them tethered. It was something more—a pull that neither of them could escape.

"Because," Selene whispered, her voice barely audible against the wind, "we have to choose. We always have a choice, even if it's not the one we want."

Cassian's breath caught in his throat, and he felt something crack in the air between them. A shift. A realization that hit him like a blade to the chest. They were standing at the precipice now, a line in the sand drawn by the gods themselves. And they had no choice but to step over it.

Selene's gaze softened, her eyes glinting with something that wasn't quite sadness, but something far more dangerous. Resignation.

"Do you understand now?" she asked, her voice trembling, though she tried to hide it. "The curse was never about us. It was always about them. The gods need us to succeed. They need us to submit."

Cassian shook his head, the words feeling like shards of glass in his chest. "No." His voice cracked. "We're not submitting to anyone."

But even as he said the words, his mind flashed back to the dance—the way the prince had led Selene in the ballroom, the way she had seemed to lose herself in him. The way the gods had always been one step ahead, pulling them deeper into their web.

Selene's voice was quiet now, barely more than a breath. "We can fight, but we cannot escape. The binding is not something we can break without consequences. It was made with the blood of the heavens."

"Then what are we supposed to do?" Cassian's voice was rough, desperate. "Just… just accept it?"

The silence between them grew thick, heavy with the weight of everything they had learned—and everything they had lost. But Selene didn't answer right away. She stepped closer to him, the tension between them tightening. He could feel the heat of her body, the way her breath caught as she stood on the edge of the truth with him. The air crackled with energy, with the unspoken tension that existed between them, the unbroken bond that stretched far deeper than either of them had realized.

Selene's eyes locked onto his. For a moment, everything else seemed to fade away—the gods, the curse, the ever-present weight of destiny. It was just the two of them, staring at each other in the cold, empty night.

"I never wanted this for us," she whispered, her voice shaking with emotion. "But I don't know how to break free anymore. I don't know if there's even a way out."

Cassian felt his heart pound in his chest. He wanted to speak, wanted to tell her that they would fight. That they would find a way. But the truth was, he didn't know. He didn't have the answers.

And that terrified him more than anything.

"You don't have to do this alone," he said, his voice steady despite the turmoil inside. "We can figure this out. Together. I won't let you face it alone."

The quiet between them stretched out, filled with a thousand unspoken words. Selene's lips parted, and for a moment, it seemed like she was going to say something—something that would break the barrier between them.

But the moment was shattered by a sound—a distant rumble, low and ominous, like thunder cracking through the sky.

Cassian's senses flared, his hand automatically going to his sword. "What is it?"

Selene's eyes narrowed. "It's them."

Before Cassian could ask who, the ground beneath them began to tremble. A low, thrumming pulse rippled through the earth, sending a shiver up his spine.

The trees around them swayed, not from the wind, but from something far more powerful. The air grew thick, oppressive, as if the very atmosphere had been infused with the weight of the gods themselves. Cassian reached out, instinctively pulling Selene closer to him.

The shadow appeared again, darting through the trees, too fast for him to catch. But this time, he could feel it—the presence— the same force that had stalked them from the very beginning. It was near.

And then, a figure emerged from the darkness, tall and imposing, its form cloaked in shadow.

"Cassian." The voice was low, dripping with malice. A voice he had heard before, once in a dream, once in his mind—one he could never forget.

"Nyx," Selene breathed, her voice barely audible.

The Betrayer stepped into the clearing, her silver eyes gleaming with something cold and dangerous. "You thought you could break free?" she said, her smile twisted with cruel amusement. "You were never meant to."

Cassian's heart raced as the fog thickened around them, swallowing the clearing. He could feel it—the choice they had been avoiding for so long was no longer theirs to make. The gods were coming, and nothing would stop them from taking what they wanted.

Selene's voice was barely a whisper, but it carried the weight of a thousand unspoken truths. "It's too late."

Cassian felt his breath catch in his throat. The choice they had fought for—was it already decided for them?

The gods had already chosen.

And they would make them pay for defying them.

# The Betrayal

The world seemed to hold its breath, suspended in a delicate moment of quiet.

Cassian's pulse hammered in his chest as he stood beside Selene, both of them staring at Nyx, who had appeared like a dark omen from the shadows. Her silver eyes gleamed in the moonlight, cold and unsettling, as though they could pierce through everything, through all the lies and the webs of deceit spun by the gods themselves.

"I thought I told you," Nyx murmured, her voice smooth, almost pleasant. "You cannot escape fate, Selene."

Selene's gaze never wavered from the Betrayer. Her lips parted, but she didn't speak. The words caught in her throat, held back by something—something she wasn't ready to voice. Cassian could feel the tension between them, a storm ready to break.

"Do you have nothing to say?" Nyx taunted, stepping closer, her movements slow and deliberate, like a predator circling its prey.

Cassian's hand tightened around his sword. "Get to the point," he growled. "We know why you're here."

Nyx's smile was chilling, a smile that spoke of ancient betrayals and secrets too dark to be told. "Oh, Cassian," she cooed, her voice almost playful, "You think you know, but you have no idea." She paused, her gaze flicking to Selene, and for the briefest moment, there was a flicker of something softer there—something almost sad. "You're all caught in a web of lies. The gods have their plans. And you," she said, turning back to Cassian, "are nothing but a means to an end."

Cassian's breath hitched. Her words cut through him like a blade, and something about the way she said it made the truth burn at the edges of his mind. He'd always known that he was meant to be part of this. The curse, the bond—he had never questioned it. But now, hearing her words, he wasn't so sure. The gods had always been one step ahead. Always controlling. Always watching.

"I don't care about your games, Nyx," Cassian spat, his voice hard. "We'll never be your puppets."

Nyx's eyes softened, just slightly, as though amused by his defiance. "Oh, Cassian," she said, her tone almost pitying. "You don't even understand. This is about Selene. It always has been."

Cassian's gaze flicked to Selene. She stood stiffly beside him, her expression unreadable, but there was a flicker in her eyes—a brief flash of something deep and conflicted. Something she hadn't told him.

"What do you mean, it's about her?" Cassian demanded. "This curse was never meant for us to control. The gods bound us together. Not to use us, but to…"

Selene's voice interrupted him, quiet but sharp. "To make us the ultimate weapon."

The words hung in the air like an omen, their weight settling in Cassian's chest. He could feel the breath leave his lungs, as though the very world around him had shifted. This was more than just a curse. It was a battle, one not between mortals, but between gods and something far older.

"We've all been pawns in their game," Selene continued, her voice steady now, though there was a tremor beneath the calm. "The curse was never a mistake. It was intentional."

Cassian shook his head, the full weight of her words sinking in. "But how? Why? What do the gods want from us?"

Selene's gaze softened, her silver eyes searching his. "They've always wanted us to become something more. Something powerful enough to tip the balance of the realms. They created the curse to bind us together, to forge a weapon from the bond between us. A weapon that would be their key to total control."

Cassian's stomach twisted with the force of her revelation. His hands were shaking, but he clenched them into fists, fighting to keep his composure. "No. I won't be their tool." His voice was low but filled with fury, the realization burning through him like wildfire. "We fight. We break this curse. We break them."

Nyx's laugh broke the tension like the snap of a twig underfoot. "You think it's that simple?" she taunted, her voice laced with a quiet mockery. "You've never seen the true cost of defying the gods. You don't know what it will take. And you won't be able to break it without sacrifice. A sacrifice that…" Her gaze flicked briefly to Selene, then back to Cassian. "One of you will have to pay."

The words hit him like a blow, leaving him breathless. His pulse thundered in his ears, and the weight of what she was saying crushed down on him. One of them would have to die.

He didn't have to ask her who would be the one to sacrifice. He knew, deep down. He'd known all along that this curse, this bond, was never going to be easy to break. But hearing Nyx say it out loud… The gods wanted them to destroy each other. To tear themselves apart.

"You don't know anything about us," Selene said, her voice quiet, almost tender. "You think we're weak. That we'll fall apart under the weight of this curse. But you're wrong."

Nyx's smile faltered for a moment. "You're wrong if you think you have any control."

Selene took a step forward, her eyes locking with Nyx's. "We do have control. We are more than the gods think we are."

Cassian could feel the tension between them, a sharp, electric current that ran through the space between them. Something had shifted—something had changed in Selene, and it made him both fear and admire her. She wasn't the goddess he had met on the battlefield anymore. She was something more—a woman who was ready to take control.

The air around them seemed to hum, the tension thickening with every breath they took. The gods had always been in control, but now, Selene was ready to fight back. And so was Cassian.

Nyx stepped back, her expression turning cold again. "You'll see. The gods won't let you win. This isn't over."

With a final, mocking glance, Nyx disappeared into the shadows, leaving them alone in the clearing. The silence that followed was deafening. Cassian could hear his heart pounding, could feel the air around him still vibrating with the lingering presence of the Betrayer.

For a long moment, neither of them spoke. The weight of the conversation hung between them, pressing on Cassian's chest like a stone. The truth had been laid bare in front of him—he had always been a part of the gods' plan. They had been using him, using both of them. And now, there was no going back.

Selene finally broke the silence, her voice soft but determined. "We have to make a choice, Cassian. We can't keep running from it."

He turned to her, his eyes searching her face. She looked as if she had already made up her mind, but the pain in her eyes told him that making this decision had taken everything she had.

He reached for her, his hand brushing against hers. The contact sent a jolt through him, the bond between them flaring with the intensity of their shared fate. He wasn't sure what would happen next. He wasn't sure what choice they would make. But in that moment, he knew one thing with certainty.

They were in this together.

"We fight," Cassian said, his voice steady, his grip on her hand tightening. "Together."

The gods had thought they had control. But they hadn't counted on Selene and Cassian's will to break free.

And they wouldn't stop until they did.

## Ten

# The Moon's Sacrifice

The forest was darker than it should have been, the trees towering above them like silent giants. The path ahead was shrouded in mist, each step muffled by the heavy fog that clung to the ground like a veil. Cassian's breath came in shallow bursts, the cold air biting at his skin. Every sound—the rustling of leaves, the crackling of twigs beneath their boots—seemed to echo louder in the thick, oppressive silence that surrounded them.

Selene walked beside him, her pace steady but her eyes darting to the shadows. He could feel her tension, the weight of the choices they had made pressing down on her. The gods were watching them now, their unseen eyes following every step.

Cassian's heart pounded in his chest, the echo of Nyx's words still fresh in his mind. The gods wanted them to break, to surrender. To make the ultimate sacrifice.

But they wouldn't.

He wouldn't let her face it alone.

Selene glanced at him, her silver eyes catching the pale light that filtered through the fog. There was something unspoken between them, a charge in the air that hummed with a power neither of them could deny. Their bond—more than just the curse—had become something else entirely. Something real.

The night felt alive, thick with the weight of their shared fate, and the tension between them only grew with each passing step. There was no turning back. They had made their choice.

"Cassian," Selene's voice broke the silence, low and steady. "Do you think we can win? Do you think… we can break this curse without paying the price?"

Her words cut through him like a blade, sharp and raw. Cassian's breath caught in his throat as he turned to face her. Her eyes were focused ahead, but there was something in her gaze—something that reflected the same fear that had settled deep inside him.

"I don't know," he admitted, his voice rough. "But I'm not giving up. Not now. Not ever."

Her lips parted slightly, as if to speak, but then she fell silent again, the unspoken words hanging between them like a storm on the horizon. He could see the conflict in her eyes—this was more than just a battle against the gods. It was a war against everything that had been set in motion long before they had met. The burden of the curse had become heavier with each passing day, and though she tried to hide it, Cassian could feel it. She was carrying something far greater than just the weight of her immortality.

A heavy sigh escaped her as she stopped walking, her gaze lifting to the sky. The full moon hung high above them, casting a silvery glow that seemed to reach down and touch the earth with an otherworldly light. It was beautiful, but it felt wrong. The moon had always been her dominion, a symbol of her power, her grace. But tonight, it felt as though the heavens themselves were watching, waiting for something to unfold.

"This is it," she whispered, more to herself than to him. "The gods are not merciful, Cassian. They will take what they want from us, and if we don't fight…"

Her voice trailed off, and for a moment, she looked as though she had seen something beyond the veil of the present— something terrifying.

Cassian stepped forward, his hand brushing lightly against hers, the contact sending a jolt of heat through his chest. "We won't give in to them. Not now."

But the doubt in her eyes was enough to make him falter. He had promised her they would fight, but deep down, he feared what was coming. The gods had woven this curse with a purpose, and no matter how hard they fought, the weight of fate had always been heavier than either of them had realized.

Selene turned to him then, her expression hardening. "You don't understand. It's not about us anymore. It's about what the gods need. They've bound us together for a reason, Cassian. We are the key. The weapon they've forged. We can't escape it."

"Then we'll find another way," he said fiercely, taking a step closer. "We'll rewrite the rules. I don't care what they've planned. I don't care what price they want us to pay."

She shook her head slowly, her eyes glistening with unshed tears. "You don't understand. If we break the curse, if we defy them, the price won't just be paid by me. It won't be just you."

Cassian's heart stopped, his throat tightening. "What do you mean?"

Selene took a deep breath, her voice steady now, though there was a tremor in it. "One of us must sacrifice everything to break the curse. If I am to be free of it, you will be the one to…" Her voice faltered, and she looked away, unable to finish the thought.

Cassian felt the world around him tilt. His body froze, his heart skipping a beat. "No." The word slipped from his lips before he could stop it. "I won't let you—"

"Cassian," she interrupted softly, her gaze meeting his with an intensity that pierced through him. "It has to be this way. The gods will never let us go unless we make the ultimate choice. One of us has to let go completely. We cannot survive both of us being free."

Her words hung in the air, heavy with truth. But the reality of it hit him like a blow to the chest. He could feel his hands tremble at his sides, and for the first time in his life, he felt utterly helpless. The love he had for Selene—the bond they shared—was far more than just a connection between two souls. It had become a part of him, and the thought of losing her… of being the one to let her go…

"I won't lose you," he said, his voice raw with emotion. "I don't care what the gods demand. I'll do anything to keep you."

Selene's lips curled into a soft smile, but there was sadness in her eyes. "But this is not something you can change, Cassian. It's not about us. It's about the balance of the worlds." She took a step closer, her fingers brushing against his, the touch almost too soft. "I'll never ask you to sacrifice for me. But if it comes down to it, I will choose to break free. No matter the cost."

The silence that followed was filled with the weight of their shared realization. The world had closed in on them, and the choice had been made long before they had even realized it. One of them would have to face the gods' wrath alone. One would have to let go.

The moon above them flickered, as if in warning. The night air seemed to grow heavier, as though the heavens themselves were watching, waiting for the final decision to be made.

Cassian's chest tightened, the world blurring around him as his mind raced with thoughts of what might come. His gaze locked with Selene's, and in that moment, he realized something he hadn't fully understood before. They were bound together, yes. But they were also two souls with the power to defy fate itself.

"Whatever happens," he whispered, his voice filled with determination, "I'm with you. We'll face this together. No matter what."

Selene's eyes softened, a flicker of something vulnerable passing through them before it was masked by the weight of the reality they now faced. She reached up, her fingers tracing the side of his face in a soft, almost affectionate gesture. "No matter what," she agreed.

And in that moment, as the air around them seemed to vibrate with the tension of what was to come, Cassian knew one thing for certain.

They would fight.

But at what cost?

**Eleven**

# A Love Worth Defying the Gods

The air was thick with the scent of rain, but the storm had yet to break. The sky above was a swirl of dark clouds, heavy and threatening, as if the heavens themselves had conspired to mirror the storm brewing in Cassian's chest. He stood at the edge of the clearing, staring into the distance, his breath coming in shallow bursts. Every instinct screamed at him to run, to flee, but he knew better. There was nowhere to run.

Beside him, Selene stood like a pillar of ice, her body rigid, her eyes fixed on the horizon. The moon had risen high above them, its pale light casting an eerie glow on her face, illuminating the silver threads in her hair. It was beautiful, but it was wrong. The moon had always been her domain, a symbol of power and grace, but tonight it felt like a silent witness to the choices they had to make.

Cassian's heart raced as he turned toward her. He could feel the pull between them, the invisible thread that bound them together, tightening with each passing moment. It was stronger now, more than just a curse. It was something real, something that went beyond the gods' plans, beyond the celestial webs they had woven around them. He couldn't quite explain it—couldn't quite put it into words—but Selene was his in ways that nothing else in his life had ever been.

Yet, even as the weight of their connection threatened to crush him, something darker loomed ahead. The gods' demands were growing clearer, more urgent, and the price they wanted to extract from them both seemed impossible to defy. One of them would have to sacrifice everything. One of them would have to let go.

Selene's voice broke the silence, low and steady. "It's time."

Cassian's stomach twisted, the words sinking into him like stones. "Are you ready?"

She didn't look at him at first. Her eyes were trained on the shadows that stretched across the forest, her mind clearly somewhere else. He knew the answer before she spoke.

"No," she whispered. "But we don't have a choice."

Cassian stepped forward, his hand reaching for hers, the familiar warmth of her touch grounding him in the midst of the chaos swirling around them. He could feel the tension in her fingers, the hesitation that mirrored his own.

"You don't have to do this," he said, his voice low, desperate. "We can still find a way. We don't have to—"

Her fingers tightened around his, silencing him. Her eyes met his, the vulnerability in them undeniable. "We've already made our choice. We have no more time."

A gust of wind swept through the clearing, making the trees shudder. The air grew colder, and Cassian could feel the weight of the gods' gaze, their unseen eyes pressing down on him. They had been watching from the shadows, orchestrating everything with the precision of an ancient plan. They were pulling the strings, and now it was their turn to collect what was owed.

He shook his head, unable to accept it. "There has to be another way. We can fight them. We can—"

Selene's gaze softened, and for the first time in what felt like an eternity, the hardness in her expression faltered. Her fingers traced his jaw, the touch delicate, almost tender, as though she were memorizing the feel of him.

"We've already been fighting," she said softly. "We've been fighting for so long, Cassian. But the truth is…" She hesitated, and the words hung between them like a breath held too long. "The truth is, we can't win this fight the way we've been fighting. The gods have too much power. They will always be one step ahead."

The weight of her words pressed on him, but he didn't let go of her. He couldn't. "Then what's left?" he asked, his voice raw with the need for something—anything—that would free them from this nightmare.

Her eyes locked onto his, her expression unreadable. "You. You are the key, Cassian. The curse—the bond—it was always meant to be more than just a link between us. It was meant to forge a weapon. A weapon that the gods would control. But you…" She swallowed hard, her voice barely a whisper. "You are more than they ever realized. You've always been more than they ever gave you credit for."

He blinked, confusion swirling in his chest. "What are you saying?"

Selene stepped back, her gaze drifting toward the moon. "I'm saying that I can't break the curse alone. I never could. But you…" She turned toward him then, her silver eyes burning with an intensity that made his heart stutter. "If you're willing to sacrifice, if you're willing to let go of everything, you can break the curse. You can end it all."

The world seemed to stop. His breath caught in his throat, and his legs nearly gave way beneath him. "You want me to…" His voice faltered, but he forced the words out. "You want me to give up everything. For you."

Selene's gaze was steady, unflinching. "For us. For the world we can create after this. But there's a price, Cassian. And I'm asking you to make it."

Cassian felt his chest tighten, the air around him thick with the weight of her words. He could feel the pull between them, the bond that had woven them together, the curse that had entwined their souls. The gods had always wanted them to break—to destroy each other. But this—this was different. This was about breaking the chains of fate, about choosing their own path.

But the cost…

"No," he said, his voice steady despite the turmoil inside him. "I won't do it. I won't make that choice. I will never let go of you."

She stepped closer, her breath warm against his skin, the tension between them crackling with an intensity that threatened to overwhelm him. "You don't have a choice, Cassian. We never did. The gods will make sure of that. But if you're willing to sacrifice, we can finally be free."

He could see the pain in her eyes, the battle she had fought in silence. She had already made her decision. But Cassian… he couldn't do it. He couldn't lose her. Not like that. Not when there was so much left to fight for.

He reached for her then, his hand cupping her cheek, and for a moment, the world faded away. There was only her—only them. The bond between them was undeniable, the love that had grown between them stronger than anything they had faced.

"I love you," he whispered, his voice breaking. "I'll never let you go."

Selene's eyes softened, and for the briefest moment, there was a flicker of something other in her gaze—something far more than the curse, far more than the gods could ever control. It was love, pure and simple. But it was also defiance.

"I love you too," she murmured, her voice thick with emotion. "But you have to make a choice. It's the only way to end this."

Cassian stood there, his heart heavy with the weight of her words. He had no answers. He had no way of knowing if they could escape the gods' grasp or if the price would be too high. But one thing was clear—they would face this together, no matter the cost.

But would it be enough? Would their love be enough to break the chains of fate, to tear down the gods' plans and rewrite the rules of their destinies?

As the moonlight bathed them both, Cassian knew that the next moment would define everything. And when the choice came, when the sacrifice was demanded, he would have to decide. Would he give everything for love? Or would they both be torn apart by the very force that had bound them?

# Twelve

## The Eternal Rebellion

The forest was silent, eerily so.

Cassian could feel it in the air—the waiting, the stillness before a storm. The tension was palpable, thick like a fog that pressed against his skin, suffocating him with its weight. The path ahead was cloaked in shadows, the trees standing as silent witnesses to the battle that was about to unfold. His heart pounded in his chest, the beat erratic, driven by a mixture of anticipation and dread.

Beside him, Selene walked as if nothing had changed. Her stride was steady, her shoulders squared, her eyes focused ahead. But he could see it in her eyes—the fear. It was always there, hidden behind the mask of her godly composure. He had always known it was there. The gods had bound them together, and now, they would take what was theirs.

They had reached the final threshold—the place where the gods had chosen to claim what they had always believed was theirs to control. The clearing before them was bathed in the pale, ghostly light of the moon, casting long, sharp shadows across the ground. The very air felt heavy with the power of something ancient, something powerful.

Cassian turned to Selene, his fingers brushing against hers. It was a small, simple gesture, but it was enough to send a jolt through him. He could feel the bond between them, raw and electric, pulsing with the intensity of their shared fate. The love they had fought for, the love that had grown between them in defiance of the gods' will, was now the only thing that could stand against the storm that was about to break.

"I can feel them," she whispered, her voice low and steady. "The gods are watching. They're waiting for us to make our move."

Cassian swallowed hard. The weight of their gaze was like a physical force, heavy and suffocating. The gods had always been one step ahead, always pulling the strings, always controlling their every move. But this time, it was different. They had made their choice. They had chosen each other. And now, nothing would stop them.

He reached for her hand, threading his fingers through hers. The simple act of holding her hand, of feeling her warmth against his skin, reminded him of everything they had fought for. But it also reminded him of what was at stake. The gods had demanded a sacrifice, a choice that neither of them could avoid. One of them would have to let go.

"I'm not going to lose you," he said, his voice raw with emotion. "No matter what happens, I won't lose you."

Selene's gaze softened, her lips curling into a faint, bittersweet smile. "You won't. But we don't get to choose who will make the sacrifice, Cassian. The gods have already decided."

Her words struck him like a blow, but he couldn't let it show. He could feel the weight of her words, but he couldn't allow himself to believe them. They had come this far. They had made it this far. And they would fight—together.

"Then let them decide," he said, his voice growing steadier. "But whatever they do, whatever price they want us to pay, I'm not letting you go. Not now. Not ever."

Selene didn't speak. She only nodded, a silent agreement, and together, they stepped into the clearing.

The moment they crossed the threshold, the air shifted. The ground beneath their feet trembled, and the very sky above them seemed to darken, the moon flickering as though it had caught in the threads of something unseen. The presence of the gods was all around them, pressing down on them like a suffocating force, bending the very fabric of reality.

Cassian could feel it—the weight of their eyes on him, on them. The gods were watching, waiting for them to fall. But Cassian's heart burned with a defiance that he hadn't known he was capable of.

The clearing before them shimmered with an unnatural light, the shadows cast by the trees growing long and dark. And then, a figure emerged from the darkness—tall, cloaked, its face hidden beneath the folds of its hood. The air around it seemed to distort, as though the very presence of the being was warping reality itself.

It spoke, its voice a cold, echoing rumble that reverberated through the very ground beneath their feet. "You have defied the gods, and for that, you will pay."

Cassian's hand instinctively went to his sword, but Selene's grip on his arm stopped him. He turned to her, his brow furrowed in confusion, but she only shook her head. "It's not him," she whispered. "It's the gods themselves."

The figure stepped forward, revealing its true form—or rather, its lack of form. It was a shadow, a being of pure darkness, its body shifting and changing like liquid, its presence far more terrifying than any mortal enemy.

"You have no idea what you have done," the shadow said, its voice like the rustle of dead leaves. "The curse that binds you was never meant to be broken. The gods will never forgive you for defying them."

Cassian felt the weight of its words, but he stood his ground. "I don't care what the gods think." His voice rang with defiance, but beneath it, there was a tremor. A fear he couldn't quite control.

Selene's grip on his hand tightened, her voice steady despite the tension in the air. "The gods can't control us anymore. We've broken their chains."

The shadow lunged forward, faster than Cassian could react. He barely had time to draw his sword before it was upon them, its tendrils of darkness reaching for them both, a coldness that stole the very air from his lungs.

But before it could touch them, Selene moved.

She raised her hand, her fingers glowing with an otherworldly light, a light that seemed to push back the darkness itself. The shadow hissed, recoiling, as if repelled by the very force that Selene had unleashed. Cassian could feel the power surging through her, a power he had never seen before—raw, untamed, and beautiful in its destructive force.

"You cannot break us," Selene said, her voice rising above the chaos. "We are more than your puppet, more than your weapon. We are free."

The shadow shrieked, a sound like the cracking of a thousand shattered worlds, as it retreated into the darkness from which it had come.

Cassian watched, breathless, as the night fell into a sudden, unnatural stillness. The clearing was bathed in an eerie calm, the tension dissipating as quickly as it had arrived.

Selene's hand slipped from his arm, and she took a step back, her eyes flickering with a mixture of exhaustion and relief. "It's over," she whispered, but the words seemed to hang in the air, fragile, like a promise that had yet to be fulfilled.

Cassian stepped toward her, his chest still tight with the remnants of fear, the adrenaline still coursing through his veins. "We did it," he said, his voice hoarse with disbelief. "We broke it."

Selene didn't respond immediately. Instead, she looked up at the sky, her eyes searching for something in the darkness. The moon was still there, its light pale and distant, but it felt different now. As if the heavens themselves had shifted in response to their defiance.

She turned back to him, her gaze softening, the faintest hint of a smile tugging at her lips. "We did it," she agreed, but her voice held something more—something that Cassian couldn't quite place.

And then, she reached for him. Her fingers brushed his cheek, and for the first time in what felt like an eternity, Cassian allowed himself to believe that they had done it. That they had won.

And in that moment, the weight of their bond—the love that had tied them together—was finally free.

But as they embraced beneath the fading light of the moon, Cassian couldn't shake the feeling that the gods' wrath wasn't finished.

The war had just begun.